SEPTEMBER 50 COLORING PAGES FOR ADULTS RELAXATION

SHIH CHIEN HUA

PUBLISHED BY:
SHIH CHIEN HUA
Copyright © 2018

SEABIRD SHOP >50FOR

FB FAN PAGE

Disclaimer
The information contained in this book is for general information purposes only. The information is provided by the authors and while we endeavor to keep the information up to date and correct, we make no representations or warranties of any kind, express or implied, about the completeness, accuracy, reliability, suitability or availability with respect to the book or the information, products, services, or related graphics contained in the book for any purpose. Any reliance you place on such information is therefore strictly at your own risk.

SEPTEMBER 1ST

note:

_____

_____

_____

SEPTEMBER 2ND

note:

_____

_____

_____

SEPTEMBER 3RD

note:

_____

_____

_____

SEPTEMBER 4TH

note:

_____

_____

_____

SEPTEMBER 5TH

note:

_____

_____

_____

SEPTEMBER 6TH

note:

_____

_____

_____

SEPTEMBER 7TH

note:

_____

_____

_____

SEPTEMBER 8TH

note:

_____

_____

_____

SEPTEMBER 9TH

note:

_____

_____

_____

SEPTEMBER 10TH

note:

_____

_____

_____

SEPTEMBER 11TH

note:

_____

_____

_____

SEPTEMBER 12TH

note:

_____

_____

_____

SEPTEMBER 13TH

note:

_____

_____

_____

SEPTEMBER 14TH

note:

_____

_____

_____

SEPTEMBER 15TH

note:

_____

_____

_____

SEPTEMBER 16TH

note:

_____

_____

_____

SEPTEMBER 17TH

note:

_____

_____

_____

SEPTEMBER 18TH

note:

_____

_____

_____

SEPTEMBER 19TH

note:

_____

_____

_____

SEPTEMBER 20TH

note:

_____

_____

_____

SEPTEMBER 21TH

note:

_____

_____

_____

SEPTEMBER 22TH

note:

_____

_____

_____

SEPTEMBER 23TH

note:

_____

_____

_____

SEPTEMBER 24TH

note:

_____

_____

_____

SEPTEMBER 25TH

note:

_____

_____

_____

SEPTEMBER 26TH

note:

_____

_____

_____

SEPTEMBER 27TH

note:

_____

_____

_____

SEPTEMBER 28TH

note:

_____

_____

_____

SEPTEMBER 29TH

note:

_____

_____

_____

SEPTEMBER 30TH

note:

_____

_____

_____

SEPTEMBER 31TH

note:

_____

_____

_____

SEPTEMBER 32TH

note:

_____

_____

_____

SEPTEMBER 33TH

note:

_____

_____

_____

SEPTEMBER 34TH

note:

_____

_____

_____

SEPTEMBER 35TH

note:

_____

_____

_____

SEPTEMBER 36TH

note:

_____

_____

_____

SEPTEMBER 37TH

note:

_____

_____

_____

SEPTEMBER 38TH

note:

_____

_____

_____

SEPTEMBER 39TH

note:

_____

_____

_____

SEPTEMBER 40TH

note:

_____

_____

_____

SEPTEMBER 41TH

note:

_____

_____

_____

SEPTEMBER 42TH

note:

_____

_____

_____

SEPTEMBER 43TH

note:

_____

_____

_____

SEPTEMBER 44TH

note:

_____

_____

_____

SEPTEMBER 45TH

note:

_____

_____

_____

SEPTEMBER 46TH

note:

_____

_____

_____

SEPTEMBER 47TH

note:

_____

_____

_____

SEPTEMBER 48TH

note:

_____

_____

_____

SEPTEMBER 49TH

note:

_____

_____

_____

SEPTEMBER 50TH

note:

_____

_____

_____